WE BUILD TEMPLES IN THE HEART

Printed in Canada.

Cover design by Kathryn Sky-Peck

Text design by Suzanne Morgan.

ISBN 1-55896-472-X

Library of Congress Cataloging-in-Publication Data

Murfin, Patrick, 1949–
        We build temples in the heart : meditations/by Patrick Murfin.
            p. cm.
        ISBN 1-55896-472-X (alk. paper)
        1. Meditations. 2. Unitarian Universalist Association—Prayer-books and devotions—English. I. Title.

BX9855.M87 2004
242—dc 22

                                                    2004048135

WE BUILD TEMPLES IN THE HEART

Side by Side We Gather

Patrick Murfin

SKINNER HOUSE BOOKS

BOSTON

For the community of the Congregational Unitarian Church in Woodstock, Illinois, which gave me a spiritual home and nurtured me with faith and encouragement and to the editors and readers of the on-line newsletter *UUNews*, who gave me a place to share.

Contents

$\sim$

We Build Temples in the Heart

~

We have seen the great cathedrals,
     stone laid upon stone,
     carved and cared for
     by centuries of certain hands;
seen the slender minarets
     soar from dusty streets
     to raise the cry of faith
     to the One and Only God;
seen the placid pagodas
     where gilded Buddhas squat
     amid the temple bells and incense.

We have seen the tumbled temples
     half-buried in the sands,
     choked with verdant tangles,
     sunk in corralled seas—
     old truths toppled and forgotten.
We have even seen the wattled huts,
     the sweat lodge hogans,
     the wheeled yurts,
     and the Ice Age caverns
     where unwritten worship
     raised its knowing voices.

But here we build temples in our hearts.
Side by side we gather.

1

We mix the mortar of the scattered dust
     of the Holy of Holies
     with the sacred water
     of the Ganges;
lay Moorish alabaster
     on the blocks of Angkor Wat
     and rough-hewn Stonehenge slabs;
plumb Doric columns for strength of reason,
     square them with stern Protestant planks,
     and illuminate all with Chartres' jeweled windows
     and the brilliant lamps of science.

Yes here we build temples in our hearts.
     Side by side we come,
     scavenging the ages for wisdom,
     cobbling together as best we may
     the stones of a thousand altars, leveling with doubt,
     framing with skepticism,
     measuring by logic,
     sinking firm foundations in the earth
     as we reach for the heavens.

Here we build temples in our hearts—
     a temple for each heart,
     a village of temples,
     none shading another,
     connected by well-worn paths,
     built alike on sacred ground.

Suddenly the Stars

⁓

Suddenly the stars—
 unseen since god knows when—
 explode across the Arctic night.
No blank shelf of stratus bars them,
 no haze or mist obscures them,
 no scudding cirrus races the wind to hide them.
Even the fierce orange glow of pollution
 cannot obscure them.
Thus old Orion does his somersault
 across the heavens,
ursine dippers pivot, reel
 upon bright Polaris's steady blaze,
 forgotten constellations process
 with timeless dignity,
 long-lost Milky Way splatters half across the sky.
Once folk knew these stars,
 measured life blood by their glow,
 fixed on them for certainty against death and chaos,
 steered by their light where no markings showed
  the way,
 found their gods among them,
 and sacrificed to them in sacred duty.

But years have passed,
 these stars unseen, unrecognized,

3

nor even missed
amid a world of roofs, electric lights,
other things to do, other lives to lead—
      until this night,
            when they come calling
                  and change everything.

Mourning Dove Day Elegy

~

Under the mourning dove-wing sky,
      last week's snow lay thick and firm
      beneath my hurried boots.
The unfollowed hearse heaved by
      and rolled to rest by a brown pavilion.
Two workmen, mittened and hooded,
      smothered in goose down, waited
      as a thin young man, dignified in wool
      and slick-soled, opened the hearse door.
Erect, carved, and curved,
      the monument stood stolid as the century,
      a Fine Old Family lay about
      waiting perhaps the final prodigal return.
The absence of mourners did not move me—
      the shriveled flesh lay boxed,
      unknowing and uncaring
      as any idle refuse.
In my unbroken pace
      I could sing Ecclesiastes in my heart,
      ponder Fate and Providence,
      and stand for all the unmade footprints
      in the snow.
No sobbing spouse was here,
      no brother, sister, child, or fellow worker,
      no neighbor, no wave-and-nod acquaintance,

no clergy—
        all gone themselves,
        or scattered recklessly across the globe,
        or lost in forgotten estrangements,
        or sequestered in infirmity,
        waiting vacantly their turn.
Here they were not missed,
    but when the spark of mystery
    last animated that corpse
    in the final hours,
        or days,
                or years,
    there must have been
        the unheld hand,
            the unwiped tear,
                the unshared memory.
Under the mourning dove-wing sky,
    I shivered and hurried on.

Merlin Said

~

Love is the only magic—

It enriches the giver
      as it nourishes the object.
It serves the instant
      and washes over the ages.
It is as particular as the moon
      and as universal as the heavens.
If returned it is multiplied,
      yet spurned it is not diminished.
It is as lusty as the rutting stag
      but as chaste as the unicorn's pillow.
It comes alike to the king on his throne
      and the cutpurse in the market.
If you would have magic,
      place faith in love or nothing.

WWJD?

～

Outside the bakery in clear winter sunshine
     on the Saturday before Fat Tuesday,
     the license plate
     of a sleek deep-blue sedan
     asked the question—
          WWJD?

Indeed, what would he do?

The son of sweet, foolish Mary,
     who heard voices,
     and that clueless cuckold, Joseph.
The boy, sawdust in his hair,
     hands callused in his father's service,
     who lectured the sages of the age
     as if they were children.
A known associate of that John the Baptist,
     who, despite spending half his life
     knee-deep in the Jordan,
     unaccountably stank
     and roamed the dusty streets,
     hair and beard matted,
     a famous madman.
The slacker who left his employment
     to wander in the desert
     and hallucinate with hermit outcasts

who dwelt in caves
babbling about Light and Dark.
The would-be preacher
who gathered a pathetic cult
to follow him from town to forlorn town,
by turns begging and giving alms,
who fed the multitude,
who embraced lepers, unclean women, and the mad,
who walked with whores and taxmen,
and spat defiance at the Temple itself,
and who, at the end, was condemned and abandoned,
put to disgraceful death with common criminals.

Yes, what would Jesus do
if he came here today?

I can't say as I know, ma'am,
but I don't think he would
be driving your plush ride.

The Caboose

～

The janitor, pushing his load down the hall,
stopped, leaning on his hand truck
as the straggling train of first graders rounded the corner.
"Are you the caboose?"
>he asked the little blonde on the end,
>whose sunny smile faded instantly
>to blank incomprehension.

He could smell the sweet sting of coal fire,
watching the endless clatter
>of the mile-long U.P. freight,
>>waiting,
>>>waiting
for that moment when the yellow caboose
would swing into view,
and if he was very lucky,
the conductor and the brakeman,
in their striped overalls and caps,
would look up
from their perpetual game of gin
and wave out of the cupola window.

The mantle of antiquity, like Grandma's shawl,
settled on his shoulders.

Resurrection

~

From that frigid morning
  when the fog of humanity
  hangs palpable before our faces
  and that fat red sun pops
  before our eyes at the far end of
  the reaching blacktop,
then, when from the highest,
  barest twig the cardinal sings
  his whistle in the graveyard,
our hearts know resurrection and murmur—
    Yes. Yes.

We are a cold people in a cold land,
  and every creeping inch
  of yellow willow hair,
  every footprint
  in newly giving earth,
  every ratchet tap of woodpecker
  on lifeless wood
resonates with resurrection and nods recollection.

It is no wonder that in hot lands,
  perpetual in green,
  moist and ever fertile,
the natives snickered at tales
  of a hanging god,

turned on naked heels,
and ran to sensible deities
who would not abandon them
only to hound them on return
with foolish promises.

But here, at turning time,
our arctic hearts surrender
to the sureness of the resurrection
that surrounds us.
Embrace the fabulous
as confirmation of the fact
made real around us,
and in the echo of this miracle
understand redemption too,
in the merciful thaw
of our glacial souls.

What Unitarian Universalists Should Give Up for Lent, if They Observed It, Which They Don't, Most of Them

~

Pews without padding, Nature Conservancy calendars.
Volvos, polysyllabic verbosity,
herbal tea, austerity,
National Public Radio, unread books in fine bindings,
isms:

    Liberalism, Buddhism, Humanism,
    Marxism, Feminism, Taoism, Vegetarianism,
    Conservationism, Transcendentalism, Atheism,
    Consumerism, Sufism,
    for Christsake, Libertarianism,

Joys and Concerns, pretension,
committee meetings, Habitat t-shirts,
potluck tuna casserole, black-and-white films with subtitles,
petitions, sermons, tofu and brown rice,
drums, theology,
season tickets to anything but baseball,
liturgic dance, poetry readings,
pride:

    Pilgrim pride
    pride of intellect
    pride of lineage
    pride of lions
    the pride that cometh before the fall

bistros, pledge drives,
advanced degrees, spirituality,
coffee hour, sensible shoes,
philosophy, choir rehearsal,
arrogance, animal sacrifice,
gender-neutral hymnals, learned clergy,
natural fibers, string quartets,
whiteness, turquoise jewelry,
recycling, self-congratulation,
acupuncture, bird-watching at dawn,
yoga, Common Cause,
God, doubt,
egotism, self-denigration,

yesterday, tomorrow.

The Janitor's Epiphany

In the mist of a late, cool spring,
     a common workman's callused boot
     impelled the spade,
     which sliced the velvet lawn
     and turned the Black Forest cake earth.
And in time he filled the hole casually,
     as if it were any other job,
     with a young tree yanked rudely
     from its old place and flung down here
     before the school.
Satisfied and ready to turn away,
     he stopped short and looked again—
     this is a Great Thing, he thought,
     and cries to heaven for ceremony,
     for some note that life has happened here.
Yet civic virtue stilled his lips,
     lest his sectarian prayer rend a fragile peace,
     and his own reason mocked an active ear
     waiting on the supplicant's plea
     to do something, anything.
But the rhythms of the seasons echoed here,
     the shade of generation turned
     with the spade and loam—
     a Great Thing has happened
     and cries to heaven for ceremony,
     for some note that life has happened here.

Lilacs Again

~

Lilacs in the soft gray glove
    of a cold, wet morning—

"Where has spring gone?"
    demand shivering lips
    as the asker speeds
    to a cozy nest
    of cappuccino and scones.

As if spring were all red and yellow tulips,
    brilliant, tall, and proud,
    swaying with God's breath
    amid a verdant sweep,
    dappled with sun and shade,
    filtered through a glory of apple blossoms
    under a perfect sky.

And when the days pass and the gray is vanquished,
    the sun restored to its throne,
    the lilacs, past perfection,
    wilt and brown along their tips.

"Too bad the lilacs failed this year,"
    the morning voice,
    refreshed by proper spring,
    chirps with the barest trace
    of disappointment.

Counting God

"God said to Moses, 'I Am What Am'"—Exodus 3:14

～

The assured voice on NPR spoke of the man
    who made his lifework to count and name
    all the gods of India—
        every deity of tribe or clan or village,
        each rock and dunghill spirit,
        all of the many names for every apparition.
After many years he had to swear defeat,
    no one can count and name them all—
        there are more gods than Hindus.

Jews and Muslims are appalled
    and vow there is but one God
    to die or kill for.
Christians quite concur,
    but opt to slice Him into Three,
    then bind Him back together.
Some Amerinds know each tree and rock,
    each crawling thing
    is and has the Spirit.
And there are Buddhists who do not care
    if God be one or man
    or even if he be at all.

This quibble over name and number
      engages a murderous passion,
    a lethal zeal and worse—
          stands between Is What Is,
         and us, restless and lonesome.

In the Century of Death

~

They are like that grainy photo on page six
    of a million tires burning in Jersey.
We shake our heads
    and click our tongues
    with disapproval and dismay,
    reflect a split second
    before we turn the page
    and hurry on to check out
        Ann Landers,
        the crossword puzzle,
        National League standings,
        or the price of gold in London.

They are the dead,
    an uncounted century
    of waste and carnage,
    stacked as carelessly and deep
    as those tires,
    alike the castoff refuse
    of industrial efficiency.

And like those tires they earn
a moment of our passing pity
    in the rush of our busy lives
        between work and soccer practice,
            haircut and committee meeting.

Unless by accident we are near
    and a pungent change of wind
    stings our noses and eyes with acrid smoke
        and oily ash drifts
          onto our own innocent cheeks.

Credo

We believe—

    that many streams join to make a river,
    that the way to wisdom lies in an open ear and heart,
    that goodness may be pursued for the sake of goodness
    and not from fear of punishment,
    that knowing and not knowing are part of the same,
    and ambiguity is permissible.

Memorial Day

~

We need no flag snapping in a quickening wind,
     no soaring melody raised full-throated by a choir,
     no marching ranks of sacrificial sons,
     no hollow oratory by any dignitary,
     no anthem or fireworks.

Just this:
     Imperfect strangers came unto a perfect land
     and made their way as best they could,
     built, destroyed, oppressed,
     forged the chains of slavery—
     then struck them,
     passed the torch of Liberty,
     imperfectly lit and often flickering in the gale,
     in ever-widening circles.

The Ugly Bug

~

She comes for a casual stroll across
    the page of my half-read book
    on a drowsy, humid morning
    in someone else's garden,
    an object of passing interest
    in the heavy air.

Have I seen this one before?
    Such an ordinary bug,
    a bit ungainly on spindly legs,
    long body, beetle-hard wings,
    and a touch of red at the thorax,
    not very impressive really.
    Maybe the adult of some garden pest
    larvae poised to strip tomatoes of their leaves?

I close my book—
    Bam!
    and expect to see
    a smear of yellow guts on my page
    and one less vermin in the world.

But on opening—
    a faint and ephemeral green glow.

I have murdered the Fairy
    who dances in the gloaming,
    winking magic in oppressive air.

One Hot Day in August

~

We knelt, squatted, sat—
    palms down upon the earth
    under the oaken vault—
and chanted the prayer of a faraway people
    we do not know.
We blessed the land and its keepers.

While the choir of cicadas sang
    psalms down,
    psalms down upon us,
their nymphs rested beneath our hands,
    waiting a turn in another year's chorus.

Who blessed the land? Who kept it?

Justice, Equity and Compassion

~

Justice is dispassionate,
    a courthouse idol in blindfold,
    impartial in application—
    but it is also the wrathful judgment
    of an Old Testament war god,
    awakening the lurking Puritan within.
Justice is ideal,
    but alone and untempered it is harsh
    and mere retribution.

Equity is parity before God and law,
    the plea of Jefferson,
    the full-voiced cry of the mob before the Bastille,
    yet, unfettered, it is a snarling demand
    for sameness and conformity.
Equity is fair,
    but in isolation it fills the Gulag and inspires Pol Pot.

Compassion is the soul of empathy and forgiveness,
    the plea of Jesus for the adulteress,
    the revelation of the happy Universalists,
    but it is slow to recognize evil,
    and reluctant to act for fear
    of victimizing the perpetrator.
Compassion is sweet
    but, on its own, apt to flabby paralysis.

We call on Justice, Equity, and Compassion together
    for harmony and balance,
    checking each others' excesses,
    illuminating each others' strengths,
    three-in-one,
    a Mystery.

Some Tend the Tree of Life
for Jacie Smith

~

Some water the Tree of Life,
     nurturing its enveloping branches,
     which cast a cool and welcoming shade
     when a blazing sun threatens to
     scorch and sere our souls.

Some gather the audacious blossoms
     of lavender and crimson,
     azure and vermilion,
     to spread before the feet
     of the abject and abandoned
     whose bare soles have known nothing
     but thorns and stones.

Some glean the windfall fruit,
     bruised and neglected,
     and by alchemy of love
     bring us tarts and pies,
     fritters and puddings,
     jams and nectars,
     beyond imagination.

Some take the inevitable autumn drop,
     melancholy ochre tumbling
     in foreboding gales,

and do not smudge the sky
with their funeral pyres
but turn mulch to humus
and nourishment for another season.

Some tend the Tree of Life
and we are their grateful heirs.

The Moon
for Danielle

⁓

The moon, fallen past full,
    rose red, blood red,
    late in the summer sky,
    a mourning moon,
    a keening moon—
        a beloved child is dead.

In the gray dawn
    the self-same moon
    shimmers silver
    from the acme of the sky,
    finding a hole in the morning clouds.

The sun will rise
    and burn away those clouds;
    the moon, bright moon,
    will fade against the brilliance of the sky.

And in the moon,
    which waxes and wanes,
    rises and falls,
    wanders the heavens,
    plays hide and seek
    with the wind and the clouds,
    she lives yet—

a changing and ever-beloved
memory.

Oh, the moon,
"the ever constant moon."

Leaving Sandstone, August 1973

~

Oh, how I yearned for
    Tom Joad's bright orange boots
    that clear yellow morning
    when they opened the door
    and I walked across the clipped lawn
    to await the bus to town.

They gave me plastic pimp shoes,
    stacked heels, two-tone brown and black,
    and light-green polyester slacks,
    a clinging rayon shirt,
    and the cast-off jacket half
    of a sky-blue leisure suit
    stitched white with pendulous collar
    and buttons the size of half-dollars.

I had begged them for my work boots,
    sturdy black, laced tight to the shin,
    surplus GI hand-me-downs for cons.
Look, I said, I'm a factory hand,
    I'll need these as a former felon
    to become a useful citizen again,
    but they shook their heads
    and handed me those dimestore disco booties.

Through two airports I hobbled
      on blistered, bloodied feet
      until at the far end of a sizzling
      stretch of O'Hare parking lot, safe at last in
         Cecilia's Bug,
      I chucked those damn shoes,
      as useless and painful as half-stricken fetters,
      into the first wire basket we found.

We Gather as Leaders
A Chalice Lighting

~

We gather as leaders, as servants.
We gather as ears, as voices.
We gather as memory, as hope.
We gather as family, as pilgrims.
We gather as faithful, as skeptics.
We gather as objects, as subjects.
We gather as wisdom, as folly.
We gather as action, as reflection.
We gather as many, as one.

As we are, we shall be.
    As we serve,
        so shall we lead.

Rainbows
for Glenn Hertel

~

Rainbows are not enough—

> They are only shattered light
> played ephemerally
> across a temporary sky.
>> Rainbows, however beautiful,
>> are erased by the turning of the head.

You have not faded with the shifting sun.

You have lingered,
> touched our lives and hearts,
> changed us with your love,
> etched the very cornerstone
> of our temple with new purpose.

Rainbows are not enough.

Migrations

~

Later they will come,
    the legions of Canada
    on the edge of cutting cold,
    backs scraping stratus slate,
    arrayed in military majesty,
    dressed in ranks and counting cadence,
    squadron after squadron, an air armada,
    single-minded in their migratory mission.

But now,
    when September sun lingers and
    lengthened shadows hint ferocity to come,
    the first glints of gold and black flit
    with seeming aimlessness,
    pushed here and there by the faintest zephyr,
    the pioneers of a nation,
    descended from Alberta prairie
    and Minnesota lakes.

One will linger
    briefly on my shoulder
    if I am blessed, then be off again.

Then if she is lucky,
    she will pause to rest with
    millions along the bend of Rio Grande

before finding a winter's respite of death
amid deep Mexican forests.

And it will turn again next spring—
egg to larva,
larva to pupa in silken slumber,
pupa to Monarch,
Monarch to migration.

Oh ye proud Canada,
mute your boastful blare—
the mighty bow before true courage.

The Dead of 9/11 Leave a Message

~

The Dead cry out—
It is not lonely here.
    They come by the scores
        and by the thousands
        every day,
        as they have always come,
        each soul here
        a tragedy for someone down there.
    They come as they have always come,
        each death a completion of a journey,
        the closing of a hoop of life.
    And we welcome each of them.

But we are not lonely here.
We do not wander silent corridors,
    our footsteps echoing,
    yearning for a voice.
We are not lonely
    for we are the Dead
    and we are everywhere,
    united in that last breath
    and in eternity.

But you Lords of the Realm,
you make haste to fill the unfillable,
    to send us more,

      many more,
      out of their own time
      as we were out of ours,
      yanked here in violence and hatred.

Let them be.
They will come in their own time.

We who know death
      do not cry out for revenge.

We are not lonely here.

Here's to You, Ralph Waldo

~

You have reached across time
    and found me dozing on an afternoon,
    reached your hand down
    and shaken me by the toe
    until I stir bewildered.

Wake up! you cry,
    the world is waiting to be noticed,
    the very autumn air vibrant with miracles,
    the incessant sun prying into every dark space
    for you, if you will see it,
        if you will be it!

The deadest of white males,
    you have climbed long-limbered
    from the pages of a book
    splayed open on my desk,
    swept your arm wide around the random piles,
    half-read volumes,
        half-completed projects,
            half-lived life that is my study
    and demanded I seize my life,
    clear my head of every derivation,
    even that from the dust of your own mouth,
    and speak at last my own revelation.

So, here's to you Ralph Waldo,
    Dreamer,
        Darer,
            Doer.

Come to Me, Sweet Jesus

~

"Come to me, Sweet Jesus!"
the TV preacher shouts,
        thumping his chest,
        waving his arms
        with the urgency and passion
        of a man whose toes
        have tapped on brimstone.

Which Jesus, I wonder casually,
        my thumb hovering over the remote
        eager to find the ballgame.

The Jesus on my childhood wall
        wore long blond hair
        tumbling shining to his shoulders
        like a Breck ad, gentle blue eyes,
        aquiline nose, a Nordic Jesus
        come to life in Jeffrey Hunter
        waiting the piercing stab
        of John Wayne's Centurion lance.

I have since seen a Jesus of every imaginable sort—
        African Jesus dashikied in splendor,
        beardless Blackfoot Jesus in eagle feathers,
        Jesus with breasts and womb,

American guy Jesus, neat-trimmed beard and
      curling hair
like the Little League coach down the block.

What Jesus does this sweating man summon
      with his electronic worship music band
      and cathedral in the parking lot,
      pews filled with rapture
      in sports shirts and sundresses?

And who, when I shut my eyes,
      do I beckon when I murmur,
      "Come to me, sweet Jesus?"
           A swarthy man,
           stocky built, barrel-chested,
           muscular forearms bulging
           from the swing of the hammer,
           matted with a thick curling pelt,
           nose large, lips fleshy,
           burnoose over raven hair,
           wrapped in dingy coarse cloth,
           callused bare feet
           black with the dust of the road.

I see a man.

Come to me, sweet Jesus,
      Let me wash your feet.

Ordination in Autumn

for Dan Larsen

⌒

A blare and wedge of geese
    rives the somber sky.
A sudden fierceness
    stirs the air.
Maples, shorn of gaudy foliage,
    weave black lattice
    against the sky.
A venerable oak
    still holds sienna leaves
    a-clatter in the breeze.
For an instant the clouds part,
    and through the apex
    of its oaken crown
    comes the sparkling sun,
    a flaming chalice
    in the autumn air.

Pictures, Poppies, Stars and Generations

~

We knew war.

Somewhere in every home a handsome young man
  peered from a tinted photograph,
  overseas cap at a jaunty angle,
    or the fifty-mission crush,
    or the crisp, square, white beanie of a gob,
  usually someone's dad in some other life,
  but sometimes the ghost of someone frozen in time,
  caught in that picture like a fly in amber
  while bloody shreds were left draped on barbed wire
  ten feet from low water on an anonymous beach,
  or splattered on the glass of the ball turret
  of a Mitchell bomber spiraling for an appointment
  with a German potato field,
  or bobbing in a sea of burning oil, naked and parboiled.

We knew pity.

The veterans in neat blue uniforms,
  sleeves pinned to shoulders, ears shot away,
  noses burned off, faces twitching,
fistfuls of red paper poppies in one hand,
  shaking white cans for nickels with the other
on every street corner, May and November,
  and no decent man or woman passed

44

without emptying pockets of change,
twisting flowers into buttonholes, onto purse straps,
without ever looking the peddler in the eye.

We knew death.

Inside scrapbooks with brittle pages and fading ink,
kept far up in the front hall closet behind hatboxes
surrounded by last winter's scarves and mittens,
between the leatherette boards bound by black
shoelaces
amid the ration coupons, V-mails,
postcards from exotic ports, Brownie snapshots,
campaign maps, and yellow clippings, a small fringed
flag, white edged in red and blue,
a gold star in the center.

In the neighborhood, we looted footlockers and duffel bags,
saved our allowances for forays to the Army/Navy Store,
outfitted ourselves in helmet liners, webbed belts,
canteens and mess kits, cast-off khaki and drab,
and amid the prairie burrs and grasses,
between the wild rose hedge and lilac caves,
on top of the carport and in the window wells,
every summer day we tried to sort glory
from horror.

We knew war and pity and death.
We thought.

And then—suddenly—it was our turn for real.

Mid-November Dawn

~

The time has come,
    I know, I know.

The soft frosts that fade
    at the first blush of light
    are over.
    The grass snaps now
    with each step,
    and the cold seeps around
    the buttons of my coat,
    up my sleeves,
    and down my neck.

Of a sudden the leaves,
    just yesterday the glory
    of the season,
    are shed in heaps and drifts.
    The bare arms that held them
    shiver in the dawn.

Long clouds of starlings
    swirl and trail across
    the lowering sky.
    Crows clamor over
    the carrion earth.

The time has come,
　　　I know, I know.

But just when the wail of grief
　　　wells in my throat,
　　　the keening for utter loss
　　　　　that crowds my senses
　　　　　　　and my soul—
　　　a simple doe ambles unconcerned
　　　across the scurrying road
　　　into a remnant patch of wood,
　　　somewhere just out of sight
　　　the half-maddened stag
　　　thrashes in the brambles.

The time has come,
　　　I know, I know.

My blood quickens in the cold,
　　　death falls away.

Healing

In the deepest cave where no light seeps,
  where cold and damp prevail,
  recall your blessings.

Among the blind albinos
  and the skuttering things
  that trespass upon your cheek,
  bring back the brush of her lips.

Deafened by the echoing
  pong.

  pong.

  pong.

  of water eating limestone,
  remember wind in the aspens.

Wrapped in the fetid stench
  of the leavings of a million bats,
  recollect bacon at sunrise.

Lost in the blackest maze,
  bring to mind each cracked and canted
   cement square of the sidewalk
    leading
     home.

The Second Coming
from a woodcut by Eichenberg

~

The ragged man shivered in the raw evening,
      pulled the blanket close around him,
      and eyed the tall man in the line ahead.

"Say, I know you.
      You're that Jesus."

The tall man said nothing.

"So you've come back,"
      the bearded man in the slouch hat said.
      "Don't you think this would be a good time
      to make with the loaves and the fishes?"

"Heal the lame!" cried the third man.

"I've got AIDS—
      touch me like you touched those lepers,"
      begged another.

The tall man looked at them
      pressing around him and shook his head.
      "This time there will be no magic.
      We must all pray
      for a miracle in the hearts of humanity."

49

AIDS Advent Sunday

～

We light a candle and await,
    await the coming of light and hope,
    the promise foretold, fulfilled.

We light a candle and await,
    await the pealing of the bells in joy triumphant,
    where now they toll in somber mourning.

We light a candle and await,
    await the hour of reunion,
    prodigal and patriarch alike embraced,
    alike forgiven,
    all that was sundered made whole again.

We light a candle and await,
    await the gifts a million shortened lives
    could have wrapped for us
    and our delight at their discovery.

We light a candle and await,
    await the day the Quilt at last is finished,
    can be lovingly folded and nestled in cedar,
    and taken out only on cold nights
    to wrap us in the warmth of remembrance.

We light a candle and await.

An Honor to Be Alive

This happenstance assemblage of atoms,
    this collection of random stardust
    echoing an explosive moment of creation,
    this unlikely bag of seawater, carbon, and stone,
    oddly and inexplicably ambulatory,
    miraculously sees and recognizes you,
    the very you seeing and recognizing.

It is an honor to be alive.

Miracle of Light

~

When the sky has swallowed the sun,
    left us in icy darkness
    save the brief gray memory of light
        escaping from its stifled yawn. . . .

When hope and heat and harvest
    have been banished into night,
    and dread, despair, and death
    grip our forlorn hearts. . . .
        Then, just then, a light returns.

Druidic fires on tors and hilltops
    call again the sun,
        and shyly it comes once more.

The awful gloom of tyranny
    is banished by a zealous few
    so that a Temple drop of Maccabean oil
        may burn a mystic week.

Some tell of a sudden brilliant star,
    a nova in Judean skies,
    to mark a coming messenger
        of hope and faith and love.

And though the gloom may crowd us still,
    the light may lift our hearts
    until this spinning, turning ball
    carries us around the sun
        and brings us again to Spring.

Let Us Be That Stable

~

Today, let us be that stable,
    let us be the place
    that welcomes at last
    the weary and rejected,
    the pilgrim stranger,
    the coming life.

Let not the frigid winds that pierce
    our inadequate walls,
    or our mildewed hay,
    or the fetid leavings of our cattle
    shame us from our beckoning.

Let our outstretched arms
    be a manger
    so that the infant hope,
    swaddled in love,
    may have a place to lie.

Let a cold beacon
    shine down upon us
    from a solstice sky
    to guide to us
    the seekers who will come.

Let the lowly shepherd
        and all who abide
        in the fields of their labors
        lay down their crooks
        and come to us.

Let the seers, sages, and potentates
        of every land
        traverse the shifting dunes,
        the rushing rivers,
        and the stony crags
        to seek our rude frame.

Let herdsmen and high lords
        kneel together
        under our thatched roof
        to lay their gifts
        before Wonder.

Today, let us be that stable.

Invitation

~

Here, let me put my thumb in your eye
  that you may see.
Let me thrust my foot to trip you as you rush by
  that you may examine the soil.
Let me drive you until sweat soaks your shirt
  that you may shuck lazy complacency.

Oh, we will have our moments
  lying in the fresh grass together
  watching the face of god
  scud by in fleecy clouds.
Together we will know illumination.

But there is more to life
  than transcendental moments
  (however wonderful),
  times when the spirit is best served
  by thrusting arms past elbows
  into the grease pit to seize the clog.

I'm sorry—I didn't become a poet
  to decorate quality-paper greeting cards
  with noble sentiments
  in graceful calligraphy.
You have me confused with someone else.

So come if you will,
    let me kick you in the shin.
I love you.

About the Author

～

Patrick Murfin is president of the Interfaith Council for Social Justice and founder and frequent host of the annual Diversity Day Festival in Woodstock, Illinois. He is vice chair of the McHenry County Democratic Party and a former candidate for Crystal Lake City Council and the McHenry County Board, both in Illinois. As a leading figure in the McHenry County Peace Group, he has convened public readings for Poets Against the War. He is also an active member of UUs for a Just Economic Community, the Unitarian Universalist Historical Society, and UU Poets. Murfin marched with Martin Luther King Jr. and Cesar Chavez and served time in federal prison in 1973 for resisting the Vietnam War draft.

Unitarian Universalist Meditation Manuals

Unitarians and Universalists have been publishing annual editions of prayer collections and meditation manuals for 150 years. In 1841 the Unitarians broke with their tradition of addressing only theological topics and published *Short Prayers for the Morning and Evening of Every Day in the Week, with Occasional Prayers and Thanksgivings*. Over the years, the Unitarians published many volumes of prayers, including Theodore Parker's selections. In 1938 *Gaining a Radiant Faith* by Henry H. Saunderson launched the current tradition of an annual Lenten manual.

Several Universalist collections appeared in the early nineteenth century. A comprehensive *Book of Prayers* was published in 1839, featuring both public and private devotions. During the late 1860s, the Universalist Publishing House was founded to publish denominational materials. Like the Unitarians, the Universalists published Lenten manuals, and in the 1950s they complemented this series with Advent manuals.

Since 1961, the year the Unitarians and the Universalists consolidated, the Lenten manual has evolved into a meditation manual, reflecting the theological diversity of the two denominations. Today the Unitarian Universalist Association meditation manuals include two styles of collections: poems or short prose pieces written by one author—usually a Unitarian Universalist minister—and anthologies of works by many authors.